Without Fear or Favour
Illustrated History of the Hong Kong Police

Lawrence Ka-ki HO   Y. K. CHU   Henry Ming-sun HO
Translated by Gordon K. CHUNG

The Commercial Press

Without Fear or Favour: Illustrated History of the Hong Kong Police

Written by:	Lawrence Ka-ki Ho, Y. K. Chu and Henry Ming-sun Ho
Translated by:	Gordon K. Chung
Edited by:	Chris Cheung
Cover design by:	Yeung Oi Man
Published by:	The Commercial Press (H.K) Ltd.,
	8/F, Eastern Central Plaza, 3 Yiu Hing Road, Shau Kei Wan, Hong Kong
Distributed by:	The SUP Publishing Logistics (H.K.) Ltd.,
	3/F, C & C Building, 36 Ting Lai Road, Tai Po, New Territories, Hong Kong
Printed by:	C & C Offset Printing Co. Ltd.,
	14/F, C & C Building, 36 Ting Lai Road, Tai Po, New Territories, Hong Kong

© 2016 The Commercial Press (H.K.) Ltd.

First Edition, First printing, February 2016

ISBN: 978 962 07 6574 2

Printed in Hong Kong

OATH OR DECLARATION OF OFFICE

(applied to police officers admitted since 1 July, 1997)

I, _____ swear by Almighty God / do solemnly and sincerely declare that I will well and faithfully serve the Government of Hong Kong Special Administrative Region according to law as a police officer, that I will obey uphold and maintain the laws of the Hong Kong Special Administrative Region that I will execute the powers and duties of my office honestly, faithfully and diligently without fear of or favour to any person and with malice or ill-will toward none, and that I will obey without question all lawful orders of those set in authority over me.

Table of Contents

Foreword

Policing Hong Kong for 170 Years

In 1842, Hong Kong Island was formally ceded to the United Kingdom and made a British colony. It was not long before the incoming administration established a small police force composed of European, Indian, and Chinese personnel, but the Hong Kong Police Force (HKPF) only officially came into being in 1844 with the passage of Ordinance No. 5 which granted the force the legal authority to execute its duties.

The historical and geographical landscape peculiar to Hong Kong resulted in the creation of a police force which did not quite conform to the pattern across the colonies of the British Empire, but there is no denying that the HKPF was a military force in the service of colonial rulers. It had four remarkable aspects in its nascent form: It was a paramilitary force whose members carried firearms in the field and operated as a government institution responsible for the protection of the ruling class. The Force had a centralized commandership and was the sole police force in the territory with all members following orders from the Police Commissioner. The team was multi-ethnic in composition, with European personnel in executive or managerial positions whereas Indian and Chinese officers served on the frontline. It went as far as to recruit officers from Port Edward (now Weihaiwei) in Shandong, China in 1922. The Force engendered social order with a strong hand: uncooperative citizens were met with coercive law enforcement through the use of physical force.

The HKPF went through several phases in the 20th century. Prior to the fall of Hong Kong in 1941, it underwent an era of specialization by setting up departments which were tasked with different duties (e.g. Traffic and Criminal Investigation Departments), and in the process developed into a contemporary organization. When the British Hong Kong administration resumed its rule in 1945, the Force was reconvened and rebuilt. Thereafter, the Force met three severe challenges in the form of riots from

1956 to 1977. The Double Ten riots, which took place in Kowloon on 10 October 1956, exposed the Force's need to improve anti-riot capacities: the Police Training Contingent was formed two years later. The Star Ferry riots of 1966 and the 1967 riots in turn led to the formation of a specialized anti-riot force known as the Police Tactical Unit. The Force was bestowed with the prefix royal in 1969 in commendation of its anti-riot work in 1967: the HKPF was henceforth the Royal Hong Kong Police Force (RHKPF).

The Independent Commission Against Corruption was founded in 1974: its uncompromising approach to police corruption soon drew a backlash from the Force in the form of the "Police-ICAC Clash" in 1977. By the 1970s the RHKPF began introducing large-scale reforms, followed by proactive reinforcements in community engagement in the 1980s, which eventually transformed it into a professional urban law reinforcement unit with the blessing of its citizens. A service-oriented approach to police

work was rolled out in 1994, and by the 1997 handover, the Force reverted to its earlier name of the Hong Kong Police Force — as it continues to maintain a philosophy of police administration in the service of the community right up to the present day.

170 years on, the Force has come a long way from being "a paramilitary force in the service of its colonial ruler". Wave after wave of formation, specialization, Japanese occupation/rebuilding, challenges, and reform throughout the years have propelled a sea change of the HKPF into a professional urban police force whose essence lies in the service of the citizens of Hong Kong. How do we illustrate the changes throughout the hundred-odd years in a straightforward and direct manner for the benefit of the general public?

Most official documents on police administration in pre-WWII Hong Kong were lost; the Force only attained relatively comprehensive archival coverage in the 1980s, and a full historical treatment of the police in Hong Kong is no mean feat. The advent of photography, however, preserved a few instances of its history, complete with the minutiae of people's lives in their specific settings of time and space. Close examination and analysis of these photographs will shed some light on the truth behind history and its developments.

As we fielded information on the HKPF, we uncovered an abundance of photographs from its early history, including those released in official documents, by the press, or in the form of postcards. The camera became a popular household item after the war, and along with it came a torrent of cellulose from official, non-official, and private collections on the subject of the police. Some systematic cataloguing of these extant prints is all it takes to animate the evolution of the Force over the century.

Notwithstanding the many years covered in this book, the principal subject matter here is the "people" whose lives and work throughout the decades are illuminated in print. Our selection contemplates "the police" as individuals and groups who live and breathe, with the bulk of our picks showing them in the field or work-related activities. Our priority is on photographs taken by, or depicting, contributors who were at the scene, followed by private collections (photographs taken by third parties or postcards), press prints, official photography, and associated documents.

There are over 200 selected photographs and facsimiles in 30 categories over five parts, namely *The Force*; *The Training*; *Duty and Mission*; *Protocol, Ceremony and Fraternity*; and *Uniforms, Accoutrements and Buildings*. From founding to training, with differing duties across departments, and through their unique lifestyle and culture, we wish to present these people through the lens of history, with a profile shot on the changes of the HKPF over the decades which may have escaped the police historians' attention in their portraits. As the Force celebrates its 170th anniversary, we also hope that our readers will see the police in a new light – to put yourself in their boots, so to speak – and by reflecting on the real state of affairs against a confusion of general perceptions about the HKPF's operation, we trust you will agree that the reality of police history interests us all.

TROOPS OF THE BRITISH EMPIR
HONGKONG. CONSTABULARY.

Armed Indian constables and their baton-wielding Chinese
counterparts at the founding of the Colony.

1   A Multi-ethnic Force

In promulgating Ordinance No. 5 of 1844, The Ordinances of the Legislative Council of the Colony of Hong Kong[1], the colonial administration officially established what would become the Hong Kong Police Force – a place where Europeans and Indians served with the British alongside a smattering of the Chinese. It began recruiting directly from Bombay (now Mumbai) from 1861 before turning to Punjabi Sikhs instead. The article of faith that was the dastar became a common sight in the nascent organization, and from 1922 recruitment drives reached all the way to Weihaiwei (Port Edward) in Shandong Province, at the time a British leased territory.

The 598-strong team counted 89 Britons and Europeans, 132 Cantonese, and 377 Indians in 1867. By 1927, 246 Britons / Europeans, 753 Indians, 600 Cantonese and 216 from Shandong made up a force of 1,815. Belarusians were hired from 1930 as naval escorts. The figures are indicative of a paramilitary constabulary in colonial service, an alien rule that was buttressed by "likes policing likes".

Ethnicity was included in each constable's collar number, with prefix A for British/Europeans, B for Indians, C for Cantonese, D mainly from Weihaiwei, and E for Belarusians.

Indian achieved independence from British rule in 1947. Hong Kong stopped recruiting Indian nationals after the Second World War, and turned to the Dominion of Pakistan from which the first recruits arrived by 1952. Macanese of Portuguese descent were also enlisted from their native Macao shortly after the conclusion of the Second World War. The Force recruited officers from many Commonwealth countries, with Australian, New Zealander, Canadian and South African officers joining the ranks.

Pakistani constables and their family praying in police quarters during the 1960s.

Indian officers at the turn of the 19th century.

Chinese officers at the turn of the 19th century.

Hongkong, New Law Court.

Postcard, early 19th century, from a series featuring uniformed Chinese officers.

(L) Old Supreme Court Building, also known as the Legislative Council Building (1985-2011) in the background: it was originally called the New Law Court, nicknamed *daai court lau*, 'Grand Court Building'.

(R) Studio shot.

Police men at Hongkong. H57

European and British officers in front of Central Police Station.
Third left, back row stood an ethnic Chinese officer of British
nationality and police rank, as he grew up in the United Kingdom.

A Police Reserve Parade in 1916.

(T) A Police Reserve Parade held in Central in the midst of the
First World War.

(B) Shandong constables driving police vans in the postwar
fifties. Many were assigned to police emergency units given
their strong build.

Victoria Harbour, 1906. British battleships of the China Squadron were in Hong Kong to prevent a Russian attack as consequence of the Russian War with Japan. The naval base was situated in Central.

2   Aboard the Sampan

Sir Henry Pottinger, inaugural Governor, appointed William l Caine Chief Magistrate in 1842 with responsibility for law and order on Hong Kong Island; as the first Harbourmaster and Marine Magistrate, William Pedder was empowered to exercise police duties in Hong Kong waters. The water unit was nothing more than a few wooden sailboats patrolling the harbour, with the British Navy picking up the rest of the duties. Even by early 20th century, the crew made do without two-way radio, and apparently duty officers took to carrying several cages of carrier pigeons at sea, so that written notes would be 'dispatched' from the harbour to Marine Headquarters in Tsim Sha Tsui.

There was problem of Piracy in the 1920s and it became the foremost concern in marine policing. Overstretched and unable to cope with merchant vessels' demands for security guards, the Force assembled an anti-piracy taskforce of 100. Recruitment drives in Punjab and Weihaiwei was topped up with 28 Belarusians. Originally from the Siberian anti-communist expeditionary force, these war veterans were initially a private security unit. The naval escorts protected large commercial ships sailing between the Colony and the Chinese coast. The first police anti-piracy squad, comprising a British sergeant and 14 Belarusians, boarded the RMS *Empress of Canada* on 10 July 1930 for Shanghai.

All marine police vessels that remained in Hong Kong were expropriated by Japanese forces during the Second World War, and the Maritime Gendarmerie[2] was established in its wake. Earlier designations of the unit as Water Police were changed to Marine Police in the 1950s. While both the Marine Police and its land counterpart belonged to the same Force, recruitment was conducted separately until 1963. All applicants had to opt for one of the units at the recruitment office. Many citizens mistook the Marine Police as a 'marine corps', i.e. a branch of the armed forces that was independent of the Police Force. As training, facilities and management progressed, the Hong Kong Marine Police gradually developed into a professional law enforcement team at sea.

Wooden pigeon coops at the former Marine Police Headquarters in Tsim Sha Tsui. It was said that carrier pigeons were the sole means of communications between the port patrol fleet and headquarters.

Anti-Piracy Guard, founded by the Force in the 1930s. Photographed members include a British Sergeant and 14 Belarusian Constables who boarded the Shanghai-bound RMS Empress of Canada on 10 July, 1930.

Hong Kong officials observing Qing mandarins executing pirates
in Kowloon, early 19th century. The pirates were arrested by
uniformed officers in British Hong Kong and found not guilty
after trial in local courts of Hong Kong but ordered to be deported.
Once deported to Chinese Kowloon, Qing yamen (bureaux) found
them guilty by Imperial Code and duly decapitated them.

(L) Crew of the launch Police No. 23 shortly before duty at the old
   KCR Kowloon Station by Tsim Sha Tsui Pier, 1955.

(R) Police No. 3 patrolling outer harbour with stern-mounted
   machine gun, 1954.

Temporary Marine Police Reporting Centre at Shau Kei Wan
Typhoon Shelter in the 1960s.

The British military resumed control of Hong Kong in August
1945 after Japanese surrender.

Hong Kong was occupied by the Japanese forces on Christmas Day of 1941, and 'three years and eight months' of hardship followed. As the city fell, all British police officers were interned in a camp at Stanley as prisoners of war, and the Japanese *Kempeitei* (Military Police)[3] took charge of law enforcement by setting up local security teams that were colloquially known as the Gendarmerie[4]. Some Chinese police reported for duty when the situation stabilized, serving the Japanese in order to make ends meet. All locally recruited constables were made to take two months of training, mainly in basic Japanese greetings like 'good morning' and 'good night', as well as fundamentals in military courtesy such as salutations to Japanese soldiers standing guard[5].

The Crown insignia was replaced with the five-pointed star of the Japanese Army cap badge during the transition, with the officer's collar number on an arm-badge on the left, and an identification patch (Gendarmerie division and collar number) written on a piece of cloth that was pinned to the watch pocket. The first days of the occupation were marked by martial law where minor offenders were paraded, imprisoned, deported or fined. Bank robbers and murders were summarily executed: once records were made at the police station with the arrestees, they were taken to the crime scene for beatings and execution. Decapitations were later changed to firing squad, and the Gendarmerie rounded up the masses so that they could witness the executions.

Japanese defeat in 1945 was followed by British resumption of administration in Hong Kong. Some of the Chinese officers who served during the occupation were readmitted by the Force after a character appraisal, and they came to be called Police Constables Japan, or PCJ. Extreme supply shortages in the postwar period meant that the warrant cards issued by the British administration from 1945 to 1946 were still emblazoned with the Japanese seal – for Governorship of the Hong Kong Occupation – and officers wore the same Gendarmerie uniform tagged with a strip of white cloth that read 'Hong Kong Police'.

Central Police Station was expropriated during the Japanese occupation as the command centre for the Western Hong Kong Gendarmerie Region. Room 01 on G/F was its office for one Nakayama Tokushiro (trans.).

Japanese soldier standing guard in Central during the Occupation, 1942.

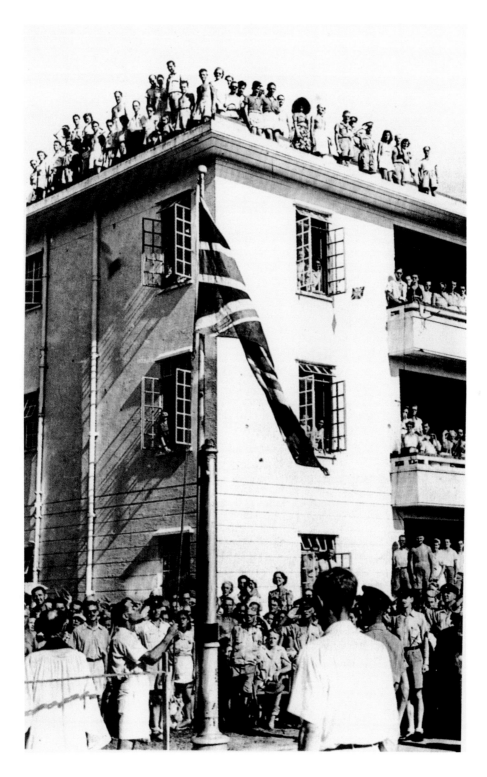

Union Jack raised at Stanley Internment Camp after Japanese surrender, 17 August, 1945.

Farewell party at the entrance sign of the Gazetted Officer's Mess, 6/F, Caine House, Police Headquarters for Commissioner of Police Roy Henry, attended by Police Tactical Unit officers, Charlie Company after the Guard of Honour at the HQ drill ground. CP Henry at third right, Superintendent at second right, Station Sergeant at far left, and the rest Probationary Inspectors. The mess has since been renamed Senior Officers' Mess post-handover, and only superintendent-rank or above may enter along with invited guests.

4   Postwar Expatriate Commissioners

As the head of the Police Force, the Commissioner of Police is its highest-ranked gazetted officer. The British resumed its governance over Hong Kong at the end of the Second World War, and Duncan MacIntosh, the first postwar Commissioner, was tasked with re-establishing the Force in 1946 as Mainland Chinese refugees fled to the city. The Police Training School at Wong Chuk Hang was completed and opened during his tenure. Arthur Maxwell and Henry Heath succeeded him in expanding the Force, with many Chinese recruited as officers and rank-and-file. The Police Contingent Camp was introduced, specializing in anti-riot operations, along with two cohorts of Pakistani officers and women officers.

Edward Tyrer and Edward Eates served relatively short tenures from 1966 through 1969, though not for want of action as the colony saw its most severe riot in 1967. Queen Elizabeth II endowed the Force with the prefix "Royal" in 1969 as Charles Sutcliffe began his term. CP Sutcliffe enacted major reforms after evaluating the aftermath of the Riots and deteriorating corruption within the Force. In order to break up the Chinese Staff Sergeants' turf wars, Sutcliffe unified the detective and uniformed branches, introduced the rank of Station Sergeant, reformed the Anti-Corruption Office within the Force, and in 1973 authorized the Godber corruption case. Sutcliffe also recruited numerous new personnel and improved police remuneration, and in reinforcing the Public Relations Bureau that was established in 1969 he hoped to improve the public image of the Force.

With the founding of the Independent Commission Against Corruption (ICAC) in 1974, Brian Slevin took over the post of Commissioner only to witness the ICAC arrest his subordinates in a massive operation; he was to handle clashes between the Police and the ICAC when things came to a head in 1977. From 1979 to 1985, Roy Henry reformed the organizational structure in the Force and established the present region/district/division hierarchy, and Raymond Anning led the transition from 1985 to 1989. Reforms in Mainland China had begun in 1978, and a growing tide of migration and logistics fomented serious cross-border crimes by the mid-eighties. Liaison with Mainland Chinese security bureaux were initiated by the RHKP as a result. With Sino-British talks sealing the deal of a handover in 1997, the Force now accelerated localization policies, and more ethnic Chinese officers were sent abroad for training and eventual supersession.

All nine commissioners from the WWII through the 1990s were professional policemen from the United Kingdom, and with the exception of Anning all had served in other British colonial police forces prior to joining the RHKP. MacIntosh stayed on for the longest at nine years from 1946 to 1954, whereas Sutcliffe was notable in his bold attempts at racking corruption, organizational reforms and endeavours to improve relations between the police and the public.

The nine Commissioners of Police, from postwar to the nineties:

Duncan MacIntosh

Tenure: 1946-1953

Arthur Maxwell

Tenure: 1953-1959

Henry Heath

Tenure: 1959-1966

Charles Sutcliffe

Tenure: 1969-1974

Brian Slevin

Tenure: 1974-1979

Edward Tyrer

Tenure: 1966-1967

Edward Eates

Tenure: 1967-1969

Roy Henry

Tenure: 1979-1985

Raymond Anning

Tenure: 1985-1989

(L) Foreign officers instructing Marine Police constables at Tai O
Police Station in the fifties.

(R) Lam Kam-chuen, the first Staff Sergeant of the Marine Police,
with three senior foreign officers at the Marine Police Outer
Waters District Headquarters, Tai Po Kau, 1965.

Two power hierarchies were conspicuous within the Force prior to rank reforms in 1972. In the lower hierarchy, the rank-and-file was led by Staff Sergeant I and II. Thereon, in descending rank, were Sergeant, Corporal, and Constable who served frontline operations and made up the bulk of the Force at nine-tenths of the entire establishment. Postwar recruitment from Pakistan and Shandong dwindled, with most rank-and-file posts eventually filled by local Chinese

in the revamp, the ranks of Staff Sergeant I & II, and Corporal were abolished. The Staff Sergeant rank was replaced by the rank of Station Sergeant.

After the revamp, the higher hierarchy of officers began at the Commissioner at the pinnacle, followed by Deputy Commissioner, Senior Assistant Commissioner, Assistant Commissioner, Chief Superintendent, Senior Superintendent, Superintendent, Chief Inspector, Senior Inspector, Inspector and Probationary Inspector. As executives and managers of the force, the posts only made up a tenth of the Force. There were proportionally more British officers in the senior ranks prior to the 1980s. While some were on secondment from the UK and colonies, the majority were directly recruited from Britain or the Commonwealth and assumed the post of Deputy Inspector (or Probationary Inspector post-reform) as soon as they arrived. New

inspectorship recruited from the Commonwealth continued after the war.

The Chinese Staff Sergeants wielded much clout in the late 1960s and early' 70s. Officially Detective Staff Sergeants I, they were only rank-and-file officers and far from high-ranking in the organizational hierarchy despite enormous unofficial powers. British officers were still running the show in their official capacity, with superior powers, positions, promotions and welfare at every turn: as Chinese police officers saw it, their British superiors were *yeung daai yan*, 'foreign mandarins'. It wasn't until the Sino-British Joint Declaration of 1984 established the handover of Hong Kong in 1997 when the colonial administration began a policy of localization, and at long last the relations between 'foreign superiors' and Chinese 'subordinates' began to change.

Farewell to Detective Staff Sergeant I Lui Lok (front row centre) on early retirement, attended by all Staff Sergeants I and II, 1968. Amongst them were Four Staff Sergeants: Lui Lok himself, Lam Kong to his left, Ngan Hung (first left, front row) and Hon Sum. Brian Welch, Senior Welfare Officer and the only foreign officer stood next to Staff Sergeant I Kwok-wai. Chan Chor-choi is at far right in the first row, and Tsang Kai-wing second right of last row.

Assembly of Staff Sergeants I & II at Caine House, Police HQ, 1969, with a number of famous names including SS Huen Hung (third left, front row), Chan Chor-choi (fourth left), Yeung Kwok-wai (second right), Ng Fuk (third left, middle row), Chan Chi-chiu (fourth right), and Tsang Kai-wing (far right, back row).

Chapter Two

The Training

Recruits

Marine Police

Riot Control

Police Dog

Passing Out Parade of graduates at the Police Training School,
1960s.

6   Recruits

Recruited Police Constables, or RPCs, were trained on campus for six months until graduation before they could assume regular duties. While the Police College itself was officially established in 1893, the training school at Wong Chuk Hang did not open until 1948, and interim training was conducted at Central Police Station or the former Mong Kok Police Station in Kowloon.

Each RPC was assigned into sub-units, headed by Inspectors and Station Sergeants, and variously trained in law, Police General Orders (PGOs), enforcement procedures, physical fitness, arms and drills. Early academies charged civilian officers[6] with instruction in Hong Kong laws and police orders, whereas Indian instructors taught drills and self-defence. Recruits in the sixties could apply with as little as a Primary Six education, but examinations were held every other week throughout the six-month period in a process which failed many RPCs with limited schooling. Failing meant that the instructor was liable to expel students – and thereby dismiss them from the Force.

Discipline above all was emphasized in the training process, and ranks were sharply underscored by instructors' all-encompassing authority and stern appearances which let no mistakes going unnoticed. Corporal punishment was still an option and the possibility made recruits both obedient and alert for fear of erring. In 2006, Wong Chuk Hang was renamed as the Police College, and RPCs now take six months of modernized curricula alongside a somewhat more compassionate disciplinary drill. Instructors will always be instructors, however forgiving they might be in the classroom.

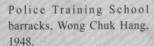

Police Training School barracks, Wong Chuk Hang, 1948.

(T) 'Grandmasters' lecturing on Hong Kong laws and police
code, 1948.

(B) Training at the Police Driving School, 1971.

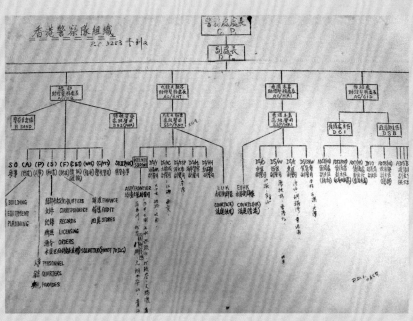

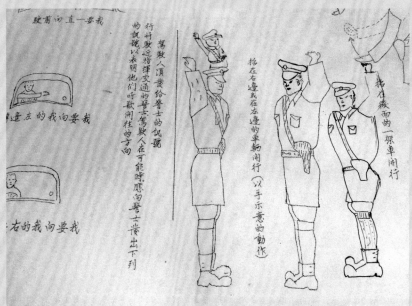

Hand-drawn notes by instructors at the Police Training School, 1961-1963.

(T) Hong Kong Police Organization Chart, acronyms with Chinese translations.

(B) How drivers should signal turns to police constables, and how to give priority.

Marine Police in the seventies.

The vessels of the Marine Police, a longstanding institution since Hong Kong's founding, were mostly manned by civilian police in the early days. Some of these civilian technicians were hired because they held mariners' licenses, and some police launches were piloted by a technical crew from the Marine Department. The deck crew were the first to receive disciplinary training in 1948, and this first cohort was followed by the first official recruitment drive for the Marine Police whose graduates became the second cohort.

1964 saw further reforms when vessel engineers were transferred to regular police assignment after a crash course in basic policing training, and upon graduation they received a posting as a Marine Police Technician. In other words, everyone on a police launch was a disciplinary officer, from captain to seaman and engineer – apart from the cook, that is.

As with their land counterpart, Marine Police recruits had to complete six months of basic training at the Police Training School. They were instructed separately before 1963 and co-educated thereafter, and marine graduates took three extra months in marine-specific training.

There were two main parts in marine police training: on the deck there was much about seafaring, law of the sea, and radio communications to learn, and professional knowledge such as technical operations of the engines. Official duties were assumed when all examinations were passed. The Marine Department accredited courses from the Marine Police Training School, which meant all graduates received the corresponding operating licenses. The latter institution was founded in 1966 at the former Marine Police Headquarters in Tsim Sha Tsui, and relocated to its new site in Sai Wan Ho in 1996.

Technical training (L) and helmsman training (R) for Marine Police trainees in the sixties.

Marine Police recruits ready for inspection at the Police Training
School, 1960s.

Marine Police Conversion Course graduation drill, 4
December, 1965.

Protestors jumping from height during the demolition of Tiu
Keng Leng slums, 30 July 1996. PTU is occasionally called to
assist government officials in land resumption.

In its infancy as a paramilitary force built to serve its colonial rulers, the Force began with little modern conceptions of riot control. Social unrests were met with full mobilization and violent suppression, alongside full support from garrisoned members of the British Army. There were no specific departments tasked with potential eruptions of riots, let alone contemporary 'crowd control' paradigms. All serving officers received riot drills against limited scenes of disturbances in their respective districts, on top of their basic riot control training at the Training School.

The Double Ten Riots of 1956 in Sham Shui Po, Kowloon and Tsuen Wan, New Territories revealed a lack of professional riot control capacities. The Police Training Contingent (PTC) was formed in 1958, offering specialized paramilitary anti-riot training to officers at Fanling Barracks, in an arrangement which proved instrumental to the resolution of the 1967 Leftist Riots. In 1968, the Force built on the PTC experience and assembled the Police Tactical Unit (PTU): the blue berets, as its members have come to be called, were now headquartered at the old Fanling Barracks.

Tactical units were divided into companies of 170, commanded by a Superintendent with four platoons of 41, each led by an Inspector in lieu of lieutenant. Every male police officer was called to a tactical unit at least once, and all promoted officers would return after they assumed their new rank. Apart from regular riot control and crowd management drills, tactical units would also stationed in districts on anti-crime patrol duties. By the mid-nineties, women officers were required to carry firearms: with this final policy on 'the great equalizer', the RHKP now sent all officers, female or male, to regular attachments at the PTU for official anti-riot training.

Commissioner's orders of encouragement, displayed at all police stations during the Riots of 1967.

NCOs from each platoon at the police training camp for land and
marine police, the latter dressed in black.

The Police Tactical Unit was formed in 1968 to facilitate large-scale riot control capacities.

(L) The British garrison was deployed to Chung Ying (lit. Sino-British) Street and got ready on the British side of the street.

(R) Hong Kong Police jointed British garrison forming an "all round defence" along Chung Ying Street British side.

Anti-Riot teams on duty.

(L) Advising crowds to disperse.

(R) Strategizing.

Frontline duty anti-riot officers during the 1967 riots. Maoist banners proclaimed "Great Thoughts, Red Flags, and Courageous Marches" in the background.

Armed officers at the Sha Tau Kok Police Training Camp (now PTU) near the border, July 1967, shortly after the shooting incident amidst tense diplomatic relations. Hong Kong Police and the British Army took defensive positions along Chung Ying (lit. Sino-British) Street which straddled the border.

Police Tactical Unit members being inspected in the sixties.

(T) Anti-riot drills in the sixties.

(B) Police Tactical Unit training in the late seventies.

PTU members training for fast-roping, 1978.

(T) Women officers called to short-term anti-riot training at the PTU
in the 1970s.

(B) PTU Passing Out Parade Ceremony, 1985.

Blue Berets C Company Passing Out in 1985, on the drill grounds
outside the Officers' Mess, or the "Smoke Signal Tower". Platoon
Four was named Best Squad.

Blue Berets C Company outside Caine House at the Guard of
Honour on the occasion of CP Henry's retirement, 1985.

(L) Police Review poster at Government Stadium, 1961.

(R) Police Dog Handler Wong Yip-wah and his charge in the seventies.

9   Police Dog

Many dog-loving citizens who thought they have already found their best friends still feel a twinge of envy at the sight of police dogs, well trained and extraordinarily obedient. Most police dogs are now imported from abroad or bred locally, whereas canine units back in the sixties and seventies were a mix of foreign purchase and local pups from citizens who didn't have the space to keep pets.

Depending on their breed and capabilities, police dogs specialized in different policing tasks. Labrador Retrievers were selected as detection (sniffer) dogs for their docile agility and tremendous sense of smelling which was perfect for drug busts in the field. The Doberman Pinscher and Alsations tailed their handlers on patrols, their towering height and strict obedience helpful in the occasional hot pursuit or subduing suspects. Occasionally they ran searches for evidence or bodies in murders.

Dog handlers were affectionately nicknamed 'Royal Dogmasters'[7] back in the sixties and seventies, but the moniker has since faded into obscurity. New handlers apprenticed under veteran masters in the team as they learnt canine command techniques. Each handler was allocated one pup and was responsible for its feeding, grooming and hygiene; formal training did not start until a solid bond was formed between the pair.

From the age of nine months to one year the pups received one-on-one training with their handlers. Starting with simple tasks such as walk, stand, and turn, training proceeded to the techniques such as biting suspects' wrists and stop-and-searches. Trainers would also hide drugs on various parts of their bodies for the sniffer dogs to detect. The sixties and seventies had Police Reviews where two dozen police dogs, mainly patrolling Dobermans, would parade with their handlers.

(T) Detection (sniffer) dogs demonstration.

(B) Police dog training.

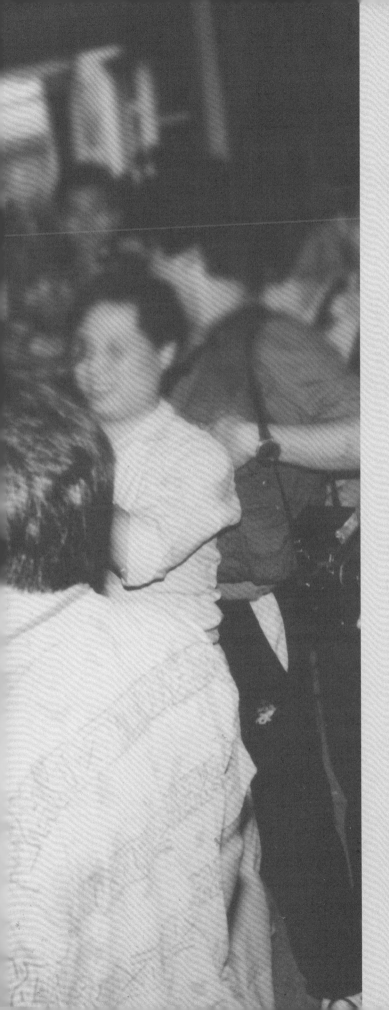

Chapter Three

Duty and Mission

Report room, 1960s, with a raised bench for officers so that
visitors must literally look up to them.

'Pass neither gates of court in life, nor those of hell in death.'[8] Some crimes will always require citizens to report in person at a police station, but the adage amongst old Hong Kong Chinese prejudiced them in favour of private resolutions. Police stations were generally a castle, guarded and forbidding place, and the report room was ominously named the *bo fong*, or the catchroom. The British settlement in Shanghai, founded in 1843, had a police station which bore similarities to xúnbǔ camps under the provincial military commander from the Qing capital. *Xúnbǔ* (or *chun bo* in Cantonese) thus became the Chinese translation for police, and *chun bo fong*, the police station. When the colony of Hong Kong was founded in 1842, the Chinese may have loaned the phrase *bo fong* for the station compound, before limiting the term to the report room.

With none of the modern open layout of the report room, citizens faced several obstacles. The front gate of the station was surrounded by high walls, and a door was reserved for citizens' entry through the reporting room. The officer on duty interrogated all who sought entry, and if a crime was to be reported, the officer would hear the case in brief before deeming it reasonable enough for the citizen to be let in.

A massive iron cage was reserved in the report room itself for temporary detention, and a stern officer who happened to be busy at the moment might order a subject to wait inside the cage until he could process a case. The interior of the room otherwise resembled that of a traditional pawnbroker, with the officer on duty standing on high behind his desk so that the citizen literally looked up to him throughout their conversation. If the officer didn't find the report reasonable, he would take the massive ruler on his desk and smack the citizen in the head.

Marine Police report room.

Marine Police report room interior, 1977.

The raised bench was gone by the turn of the seventies, and
citizens could even report crimes, seated and seeing eye to eye.
The Miscellaneous Report Book (MRB), or "Big Book", as it
came to be called in Cantonese, sat at the table for duty officers
and logged all reports.

授權狀

為根據香港法例第一三四章即危險藥物條例授權行使該章第十三條第一及第二項所規定之一切權力事

李醫務衞生總監

茲授權香港警務處督察及督察以上階級之警官行使危險藥物條例第十三條第一及第二項所規定之一切權力

香港醫務衞生總監
鄧炳輝簽署

一九六三年十月七日

Search warrant signed by Dr Teng Pin-hui, Director of Medical and Health Services, in 1963 per Cap 134 Dangerous Drugs Ordinance, s. 13 (1,2), authorizing officers of inspector rank or above to exercise powers.

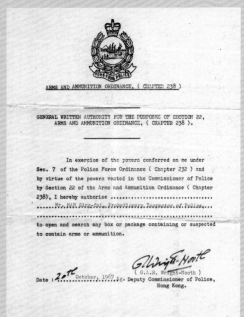

ARMS AND AMMUNITION ORDINANCE, (CHAPTER 238)

GENERAL WRITTEN AUTHORITY FOR THE PURPOSES OF SECTION 22, ARMS AND AMMUNITION ORDINANCE, (CHAPTER 238).

In exercise of the powers conferred on me under Sec. 7 of the Police Force Ordinance (Chapter 232) and by virtue of the powers vested in the Commissioner of Police by Section 22 of the Arms and Ammunition Ordinance (Chapter 238), I hereby authorise

Mr. NNN Silverfox, Probationary Inspector, of Police,

to open and search any box or package containing or suspected to contain arms or ammunition.

Date : 20th October, 1969.

(G.A.R. Wright-Nooth)
Ag. Deputy Commissioner of Police,
Hong Kong.

Search warrant by Arms and Ammunitions Ordinance as empowered by the Police Force Ordinance.

保護婦孺條例（即香港法例第二一三章）

關於香港授權執行本條例第十六條之規定事

本副處長為執行警察條例（即香港法例第二三二章）第七條行授于本人人文權力及遵照保護婦孺條例（即香港法例第二一三章）第十六條行授于不低於警長級警官之權力，予以執行。

將保護婦孺條例（即香港法例第二一三章）第十六條行使予拾拾處處長之權力起見，茲特授權

香港警拾處副處長

一九六 年   月   日

保護婦孺條例（即香港法例第二一三章）

第十六條

凡屬職級不低於警長之任何人等身為經警拾處處長以書面作普通授權者或聖由社會福利署署長必書面之任何人員，如有理由相信在水上或陸上之任何地方係用作娼妓或歧基或有理由相信該等地方係有違犯本條例之情事發生者，則毋須預先通知而得隨時入內，並來而見及質問寓居該處之任何人或一切人等。

1960s warrant template issued by the Deputy Commissioner of Police according to Protection of Women and Juveniles Ordinance Cap 213 s.16. (full text on left), authorizing officers ranked sergeant or above to enter premises without notice on grounds of suspected prostitution.

11   Warrants

In the 1950s and '60s, all Inspector and some Sergeants were issued various search warrants from the Force and relevant government departments[9] to facilitate their daily duties. These included warrants issued for the search of firearms, ammunitions and explosives in accordance with the Police Force Ordinance[10], against human and sex trafficking per Protection of Women and Juveniles Ordinance[11], and for restaurant hygiene inspections per Public Health Ordinance[12]. In those days, Inspectors and Sergeants would carry these warrants with them at all times as they led subordinates to different venues on duty. A retired officer who used to be stationed at Central recalled carrying a warrant for banks, as they were regularly inspected for adherence to their banking license conditions.

The Police Supervision Ordinance was passed in 1956, leading to the formation of the Police Supervision Section which executed police supervision orders on individuals. There were four categories, the first group were returning deportees newly detained under revised deportation regulations, which led to fixed-term supervision orders in lieu of re-deportation. The second group were detained deportees who applied for extraordinary leave to remain, which was subsequently approved by the Governor in Council contingent on fixed-term supervisions. The third was a probation-like arrangement post-incarceration, whereas this last category were convicted persons who were sentenced to police supervision orders.

Those under police supervision orders were first sent to the Police Supervision Section at the Headquarters where the duty officer would issue them with a police supervision report file[13]: requirements of weekly reports at designated stations in the neighbourhood may be relaxed to one every other week for good behaviour. After a year or so, a monthly report may suffice. The Section was dissolved in 1982, and the Correctional Services Department took up supervision of offenders thereafter.

The Immigration Department took over customs duties from the Force after its founding in 1958 although due to security concerns the Force continued to man Lo Wu until 1965. It was none too easy for the average Hong Konger to apply for a passport in order to leave the city, as *only jus soli* British subjects born in Hong Kong[14], endorsed by another British subject and armed with solid justifications, had a chance. Most local residents born in Mainland China could not apply for one, and opted for re-entry permits instead.

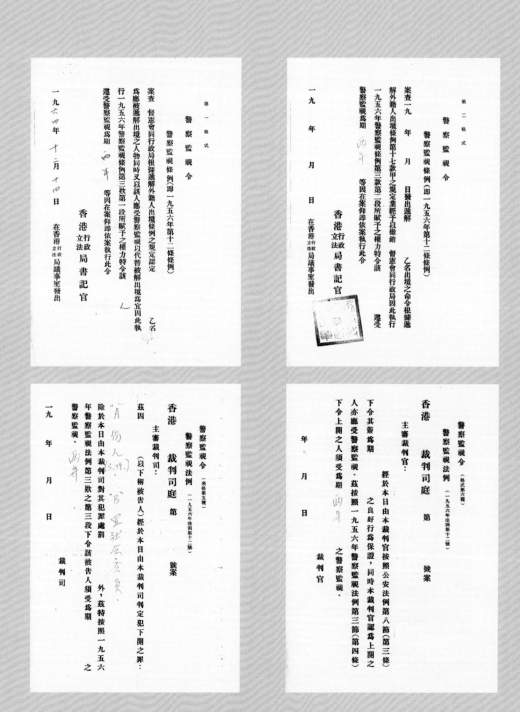

第一格式

警察監視令

警察監視條例（即一九五六年第十二條例）

案查　督憲會同行政局根據遞解外籍人出境條例之規定認定
為應被遞解出境之人物同時又以該人應受警察監視以代替被解出境為宜因此執
行一九五六年警察監視條例第三款第一段所賦予之權力特令議
遵受警察監視為期　兩年　等因在案仰即依案執行此令

香港立法局書記官

　　　乙名

一九六四年 十二月十四日 在香港立法局議事室發出

第二格式

警察監視令

警察監視條例（即一九五六年第十二條例）

案查一九　年　月　日發出遞解
解外籍人出境條例第十七款甲之規定業經予以撤銷　督憲會同行政局因此執行
一九五六年警察監視條例第三款第二段賦予之權力特令議
警察監視為期　兩年　等因在案仰即依案執行此令

　　　乙名出境之命令根據遞

　　　遵受

香港立法局書記官

警察監視令（表格第五號）
（一九五六年法例第十二號）

香港 裁判司庭 第　號案

主審裁判司：

（以下稱被告人）經於本日由本裁判司判定犯下開之罪：

茲因

除於本日由本裁判司對其犯罪處罰
外，茲特按照一九五六
年警察監視法例第三款之第三段下令該被告人須受為期
之
警察監視・　兩年

一九　年　月　日

裁判司

警察監視令（格式第六號）
（一九五六年法例第十二號）

香港 裁判司庭 第　號案

主審裁判官：

經於本日由本裁判官按照公安法例第八節（第三條）
之良好行為保證，同時本裁判官認為上開之
人亦應受警察監視。茲按照一九五六年警察監視法例第三節（第四條）之
警察監視。

下令其簽為期

下令上開之人須受為期　兩年　之警察監視。

一九　年　月　日

裁判官

Police Supervision Order forms, per Schedule of Police Supervision Ordinance, 1956. All were for a two-year period. Forms 1 and 2 (top) were issued by the Secretariat of the Executive Council, replacing and revoking earlier deportation orders under subsection 1 and 2 respectively. Forms 3 and 4 were issued by Magistrates, the former in addition to unknown penalties for assault and triad association, the latter alongside a binding-over order.

(T) Re-entry permit for multiple entry from Mainland China to Hong Kong within six months from date of issue, 1957.

(B) Re-entry permit for multiple entry from Mainland China and Macao to Hong Kong within twelve months from date of issue, 1962.

'Red Shoulder means English speaking officer,' collar number pins.

12   Street Beat Patrols

These days, nighttime street patrols usually take a pair of uniformed constables in what is called the 'twin' or double beat. The arrangement was unheard of in the sixties, and a solo constable would head for various visiting books on foot instead. Each was charged with a specific patrol zone, and if a colleague couldn't make it to the neighbouring 'beat duty', the PC would have to spread himself between two or even three beats in one go.

Without beat radios, any emergencies on the field which required reporting to a superior often meant borrowing a telephone from the corner shop. At night or in remote areas, constables resorted to the police phone box: a special key opened the box and a hand-cranked telephone was hardwired to the station. The method stuck until the advent of two-way radios, nicknamed Lil' Robocons[15], in the seventies.

Officers who joined the Force after the mid-nineties may have heard of 'Red Shoulders' without having ever seen one on patrolling officers. The unofficial term referred to a red plastic sheet or felt underneath the shoulder numbers of uniformed constables and sergeants. Red Shoulders spoke and wrote conversational English at an elementary level. It made things easier for foreigners who needed help from English-speaking police officers, especially in tourist districts.

The Government set various levels of English language proficiency through public examinations, with Level 4 roughly equivalent to Secondary 1 in the 21st century, and Level 10 was that of a sixth-former. Level 6 merited a Red Shoulder from the Force along with a special one-off bonus. The system came to an end with a new requirement for a pass in HKCEE English Language, and Red Shoulders eventually vanished from the streets.

Constables relied on police phone box on night duty or in remote areas before the advent of two-way radios or pagers.

73

Traffic Pagodas at the turn of the sixties.

Triumph motorcycles were used for traffic patrols in the fifties
and sixties.

Regional Command and Control Centre-HongKong Island, established in mid-1970s. Wong Leung Kam-san made many records for female officers, in addition to her being the first female Chinese Chief Superintendent.

(T) 999 Emergency Call vehicle command and control centre. The hotline itself was established after the WWII.

(B) Temporary Command Centre at a school next to Che Kung Temple during the Lunar New Year Che Kung Temple crowd management operation in 2007.

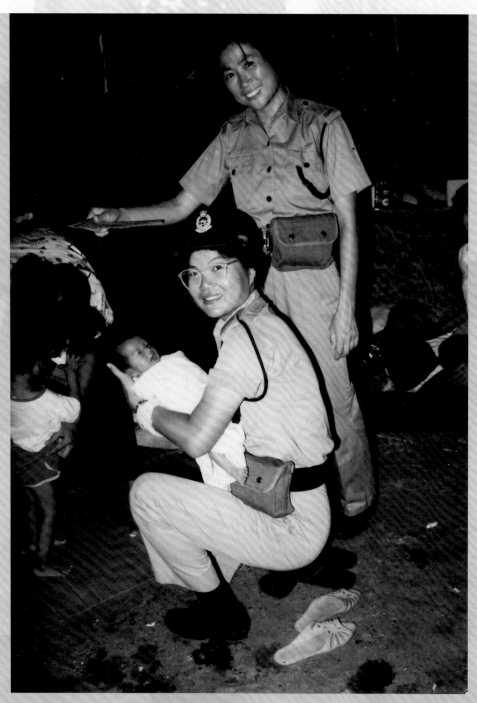

Vietnamese boat people refugee centre at Tai Nga Chau, established by the Government in 1980. Officers were taking care of a Vietnamese newborn.

13   Female Police

In 1949, Kimmy Koh was appointed to the post of Sub-Inspector as the first Chinese female in the history of the Force. Two years later, she herself assisted in training ten women officers, and nine of them subsequently completed three months of training and were deployed to various stations. Management was segregated by sex in the fifties and sixties, and women officers received separate assignments but did not work night shifts, nor were they issued with firearm.

Uniformed women officers had different dress codes for different working environments. Day-to-day duties were performed in a 'Western' blouse, special-ops 'Western' trousers, and motorcycling called for half-and-half chaps. Occasionally, they accompanied government doctors on mobile clinic duty in rural areas. For this special fieldwork, they were issued with issues of purse, leather heels, grey woolly cardigan and mackintosh, as white-collar as they come and without a hint of the policewoman to the untrained eye.

The same period also saw numerous assignments to Traffic where women officers directed rush-hour in traffic standing smack in the middle of road. To facilitate the execution of tasks, women officer were instructed to wear trousers instead of skirts. Community education and tasks involving women and children were largely handed over to women officers, with traffic safety talks at primary and secondary schools and cross-district report-room duty designed to reassure residents that it was all right to report crime.

With sexual discrimination rampant in early Hong Kong society, the Force received a fair share of reports involving abandoned female infants. Women officers were often sent to collect them, arranging for social services to put them into care while serving as their temporary guardian. With numerous women, children and students mobilized in the early stages of the 1967 Riots, male officers often found it difficult to handle head-on confrontation. Women officers were duly assigned to the frontline in crowd management units in support of their colleagues. The same tactic was used when South Korean farmers protested against the World Trade Organization Ministerial Conference of 2005.

Leather handbag issued for women officers on special duty, 1960s.

The first batch of nine women police constables, training at Wong Chuk Hang Police Training School, 1951. They wore plain white shirts and trousers in lieu of uniform. The male instructor in short trousers stood next to Sub-Inspector Kimmy Koh. Second row, far left from the recruits' view was Lam Ngoi-si, collar number 5010.

Lam Ngoi-si stationing at the women police officers' office at
Yaumatei Station. 1959.

Women police officers wore a variety of uniforms for different occasions. Blouses were worn on regular duty, and anti-riot uniform (nicknamed Korean Kit) during anti-riot operations.

(L) Inspectors at a beat conference point in an MTR station, 1980s.

(R) The first women marine police officers embarking, 1977.

The first batch of women officers retrained as marine police, with
their Station Sergeant instructor.

Tai O Station officers, 1957.

Besides the Victoria Harbour and local waters, the Marine Police also policed the entirety of Outlying Islands, and officers in naval rig used to be a common sight on land as well as at sea. They frequented a few major islands inhabited by fishing communities, including Lantau, Lamma and Cheung Chau. A glance at Tai O, Lantau in this chapter shows how the Outlying Islands used to be policed.

Tai O market was one of the most prosperous settlements in the Islands, and duty-bound officers went on an 11-day shift followed by three days off in the urban areas. The commute involved a ferry from Central to Yaumatei, via Ma Wan, Tung Chung, Sha Lo Wan, etc. and on to Tai O. The Station was headed by a Senior Inspector, an Inspector serving as deputy chief, and manned by various Sergeants, Corporals and Constables. As with other urban stations, interpreters and even Female Searcher were on duty at Tai O.

The establishment included a Rural Patrol Team, with regular patrols by duty Marine Police officers on three main routes. The first covered Tai O all the way to Chek Lap Kok in Tung Chung, the second from Tai O to Po Lin Monastery along the foot of the hill and then to the top and dotted with temples throughout. The last route ran around Shek Pik, with new security detail now that a reservoir had been built.

Green pangolin uniforms and two handguns were the standard issue for the Team, and Corporals carried a rifle. The gear included a jungle hat, green long-sleeved twill shirt with trousers, canvas holster and rucksack (with two-way radio and backup batteries inside). Each police post along the way was stocked with more than food and water rations: clean and dapper uniforms were ready for those who needed a change.

Hunting trips at Tai O Station, with the 'foreign mandarin', the Chinese detective, and the 'grandmaster' interpreter, 1950s.

Rural patrol units from the Marine Police on duty in Lantau
alongside their plainclothes colleague, 1957.

Tai O Station Commander on duty in plainclothes, 1960s.

Pangolins, or rural patrol units, in the sixties.

(T) Rifle drill with Marine Police at Tai O, 1948.

(B) Village patrols by the Rural Patrol Team in the sixties.

(T) Tai O Rural Affairs Committee with Marine Police officers, 1950s.

(B) Tai O villagers bidding a fond farewell to a resident doctor in the fifties, in front of Hongkong and Yaumatei Ferry Man Fat.

Students from Leung Shuen Bay School on High Island visited Tai O
Station and boarded a launch in 1973.

Illegal immigrants (II) from Mainland China in 1979, with Marine
Police officers on MD41, a launch which began as a barge from
the Marine Department with an extra-large hull for its mail cargo.
It was requisitioned by the Marine Police during the height of
illegal immigration, and all intercepted II were ordered to sit with
their heads down, hands over their heads, for easier processing.

15 "Snakeheads": Illegal Immigration from Mainland China

Along with the firing shot of the Great Leap Forward in 1958 came People's Communes (*rénmín gōngshè*) across the rural villages of Mainland China. Failed policies led to severe famines. In the early 1960s, a wave of exodus swept the coast of Guangdong as large numbers of Mainland residents fled to Hong Kong over land and sea. Marine officers posted at the border often found bodies of refugees who drowned crossing Tsim Bei Tsui and Deep Bay. While these waters were indeed a vast bay at high tide, it was quite deceptive otherwise. Wading through at low tide when Hong Kong was seemingly a stone's throw away, the hapless ones were stuck in the muddy seabed and drowned when the tide returned. The lucky ones who managed to reach Hong Kong waters were almost invariably covered in cuts from oyster shells in the farms.

1961 and 1962 proved to be the most formidable years for the Marine Police, when each daily patrol at sea brought at least seven or eight bodies, some headless, some under the body and with limbs missing. Officers from the launch slid a canvas that was set aside for the purpose, lifted it up gingerly, wrapped it in white shroud, and photographed the body for the paperwork before setting it aside on the deck and returning to the mortuary on shore. The decade-long Cultural Revolution began in 1966, and Cantonese residents who were persecuted to the bitter end now floated along the Pearl River to Hong Kong waters. Some were tied and then thrown into the sea to drown and bloat, whereas others were decapitated, and in death they registered on their bodies the horrors they met.

The majority of II were men in the 1970s, crossing on shabby sailboats, rafts and buoys, and few families crossed the border together. Intercepted II were taken to Marine Police headquarters in batches for temporary detention before the land police repatriated them to Mainland China.

Whitehead Detention Centre, 1980s, with numerous temporary tents.

16　"Boat People": Vietnamese Refugees

When Saigon fell in 1975 to the Viet Cong, countless Vietnamese took to the seas. Throughout the mid-seventies and early eighties, numerous vessels rushed to Hong Kong waters with occupants seeking political refuge. The freighter *Huey Fong* forcibly entered on Christmas 1978 with some 2,700 Vietnamese asylum seekers and successfully landed when the Government relented on humanitarian grounds. After adopting the 'port of first asylum' policy in 1979, the city began what would become a 20-year struggle with *lan man man tai*, or "The Refugee Question".

Apart from large freighters, asylum seekers also went via Cholon, Ho Chi Minh City or otherwise smuggled their way through the coasts of Guangxi before literally sailing close to the wind for Hong Kong on rafts. During the peak, marine police speedboats intercepted several vessels with hundreds of refugees every night. Outmanoeuvred officers resorted to borrowing crafts from the Marine Department. Intercepted refugees' hands were bound behind their backs as a precaution against attacks on police personnel, and were then transferred and registered on the police craft before being quarantined at Tai Lam Chung Marine Headquarters. Having been trapped in the hull for a long time, the refugees were in an unhygienic and malodorous condition.

The earlier arrivals were usually richer. Many of them were intellectuals and professionals, doctors and teachers who were forced to abandon their homes as they fled the war. They were eager with anticipation at the sight of marine officers when their rafts entered Hong Kong waters. Most of them were hoping that they would be taken in by Western countries after arriving in Hong Kong, and eventually turning a new page in life after their final journey. Later on, refugees chiefly fled for economic reasons[16]. In 1988 the Government implemented the UNHCR Comprehensive Plan of Action for Indochinese Refugees, distinguishing *prima facie* (political) refugees from boat people and detaining the latter as illegal immigrants before forcible repatriation.

A large number of Vietnamese asylum seekers arrived at Hong Kong in the seventies.

(L) Freighter Skyluck arrived with 2,800-odd Vietnamese refugees.

(R) Vietnamese boat people entering Hong Kong waters on crude wooden
   vessels.

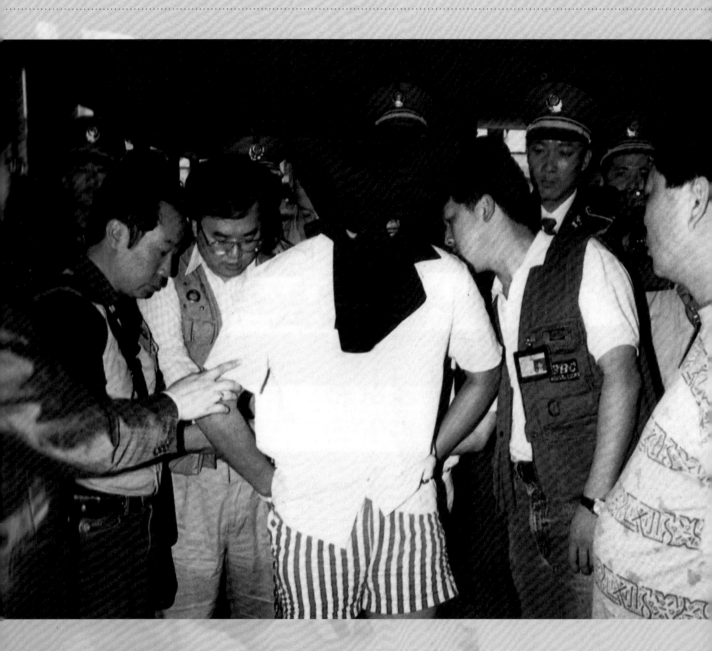

A leader of an armed robbery syndicate was apprehended in Shenzhen, China in 1992. Mainland Chinese security bureau personnel handed over the suspect to Hong Kong officers on Lo Wu Bridge.

17   Cross-border Crime

As the Cultural Revolution drew to a close in 1976, residents continued to depart from the coast of Guangdong to Hong Kong. Many illegal immigrants were granted leave to remain in Hong Kong and became the city's *sun yi man*, or New Migrants. A few of them decided to take a shot at robbing banks and jewelry shops, and this gang became known as the Big Circle Boys[17]. In the mid-eighties, local criminal enterprises began to outsource robberies to resident New Migrants; later on, operations smuggled armed Canton residents for a 'city job' before immediately repatriating them to the Mainland, much to the consternation of Hong Kong officers. *The Long Arm of the Law*, a 1984 local film, featured a gang of robbers from Canton in a veiled reference to the BCB, and the name of the film entered local parlance as a moniker for cross-border armed robbers[18].

Alongside robbers were smugglers who tuned up their speedboats into Big Fliers (*daai fei*): numerous luxury cars were stolen in Hong Kong and transported to Mainland China on these, and China-Hong Kong cross-border crimes had become the thorniest of issues for the Force at the turn of the 1980s. The RHKP realized that no solutions would be forthcoming without the cooperation and assistance of their Mainland Chinese counterpart, and early exchanges, which had started a decade earlier, were a key element in the grew into formal negotiations and conferences. Assistance from law enforcement departments in China gradually helped the Force to reduce cross-border crime in mid 1990s.

Police exchanged heavy fire during an arrest operation with armed robbery syndicates holding out in a tenement building (tong lau) on Li Tak Street, Tai Kok Tsui in 1992. The captured suspect was brought back later on for a crime scene reconstruction.

Hong Kong police officers greeted their Shenzhen security bureau counterpart on Lo Wu bridge in 1992, as a Hong Kong suspect arrested in Shenzhen was handed back to the colony.

(T) Organized Crime and Triad Bureau (OCTB) uncovered a local armed robbery syndicate with Tokarev TT-33 (Type 54 or Black Star) made in and smuggled from China in 1991. Li Kwan-ha, then Commissioner of Police (fifth left) commended officers in person at their office.

(B) In 1999, the Narcotics Bureau found 14kg of heroin in a drug bust, synthesized in the Southeast Asian Golden Triangle and smuggled to Mainland China before its final import to Hong Kong via various routes.

Expedition to the Tiandihui relic site in Fujian with Mainland Chinese Hongmen expert Fang Daojin (second left). RHKP triad experts include Kwok Shue-wing, Yip Bao-fook (second right) and Leung Chiu-yuk in the back row, and Chiu Chun-seng at the front.

18   Triad Experts

The press often mentions court evidence of so-called Triad Experts, but who exactly are these people? How did they qualify in the first place? As it is, these experts are members of the Triad Expert cadre in the Force – and naturally every one of them is a police officer, deemed a valid expert witness to be called to testify in court in triad-related cases. Why did the Force establish such a cadre?

By Cap 151 s 20 in Membership, etc., Societies Ordinance,

"Any person who is or acts as a member of a triad society or professes or claims to be a member of a triad society or attends a meeting of a triad society or who pays money or gives any aid to or for the purposes of the triad society or is found in possession of or has the custody or control of any books, accounts, writing, lists of members, seals, banners or insignia of or relating to any triad society or to any branch of a triad society whether or not such society or branch is established in Hong Kong, shall be guilty of an offence(...)"

If the prosecution makes reference to this section, it must convince the court that the defendant has participated in triad-related activities, and expert testimony thus becomes key.

The Force began the first Triad Expert Programme in 1984, headed by then Superintendent Robert Cheng and taught by veterans Cheng Wui-sing, Lui Fung-ying, Au Lam and Cheung Ka-wing. Selected officers with triad knowledge and CID experience underwent a three-week course covering the background and development of the fraternal organization Hongmen (Tiandihui)[19], the local Triad, initiation and promotion ceremonies, codes, literature, gestures, rituals, jargon and activities. Students also had to learn relevant laws, practise in moot courts, and sit examinations. Once they have completed the course, they were recognized by courts of law as expert witnesses on the subject matter and could be called by prosecutors in triad-related cases.

The most celebrated of them all, Yip Bao-fook, was styled the Walking Dictionary of Triads by the press. Yip was promoted to Chief Inspector in 1991 and lead the research unit of the Criminal Intelligence Bureau, until his retirement in 2000: between him, Leung Chiu-yuk, Kwok Shu-wing and Chiu Chun-sing, numerous Triad Experts were trained.

Chief Inspector Yip Bao-fook (second right) with Chiu, Kwok and Leung (left to right) lecturing Hongmen history with a simulated *hung ga chi*, or Ancestral Hall of the House of Hong, for students in the Triad Expert course.

Charles, Prince of Wales visiting Yuen Long in 1979, escorted by Royal Escort Group head Chief Inspector Ian Stenton at the lead motorcade. Residents welcomed the Prince along the way with Union Jacks.

1842 marked the formal establishment of Crown Colony in Hong Kong, and pre-handover police officers took the Oath (or Declaration) of Office "to well and faithfully serve Her Majesty Queen Elizabeth the Second, Her Heirs and Successors"[20] since 1952. All police buildings flew the Union Jack and displayed Royal Portraits indoors as a sign of allegiance. Both Caine House at Wanchai Police Headquarters and the longstanding Central Police Station carried different autographed images signed by the monarch. In recognition of its role in resolving the 1967 Riots, the Force was bestowed with the title of "Royal" and Her Majesty's cousin Princess Alexandra, The Hon. Lady Ogilvy, as its honorary Commandant General.

In 1975, HM The Queen and husband HRH The Prince Philip, Duke of Edinburgh paid their first visit to Hong Kong, boarding the official yacht *The Lady Maurine* at Tsim Sha Tsui Public Pier and arriving at Queen's Pier across the Victoria Harbour. The two revisited the Colony en route to China in 1986. Their children, Charles, Prince of Wales, Anne, Princess Royal, Prince Edward, Earl of Wessex and Prince Andrew, Duke of York, all visited the city, as did other members of the royal family, including Diana, Princess of Wales and Princess Alexandra. Each of these visits entailed considerable police manpower and security detail, and the RHKP kept close correspondence with the British garrison[21], the Ministry of Defence, and the Secret Intelligence Service (MI6) for maximum protection. A 15-strong Royal Escort Team was formed in April 1986 for Princess Alexandra's visit, taking over various duties from the old escort that were Traffic Department at Hong Kong Island District and Police Driving School. The team was renamed the Force Escort Group after the handover.

The Governor of Hong Kong was appointed by the monarch of the United Kingdom as her representative, and exercised royal prerogative as head of administration and commander-in-chief, with an exalted rank and overarching powers. All Governors were British and, with the exception of Chris Patten, largely sealed off from the public eye. 'Governors' meeting the public were one way to catch a glimpse of the man.

Often seen shadowing the Governor was an *aide-de-camp* ("assistant in the field"), a serving Superintendent-rank officer who had passed the most stringent vetting procedures. The personal assistant tended to be a high-flyer in the Force, and the post was invariably filled by non-Chinese police officers until the handover.

Royal Hong Kong Police
Oath/Declaration of Office
皇家香港警務處
就職宣誓書/宣言

"**You**, (HO Ming-sun) took the Oath or Declaration of office
to well and faithfully serve Her Majesty Queen Elizabeth II,
Her Heirs and Successors, according to law as a Police Officer,
to obey, uphold and maintain the law of the Colony of Hong Kong,
to execute the Powers and duties of office honestly, faithfully
and diligently, without fear or favour to any person and with
malice or ill will toward none, and to obey without question
all lawful orders of those set in authority over you."

『閣下 何明新 於一九七六 年 十 月 十一 日
宣誓就職，以警務人員身份，願依法竭誠效忠
英女皇陛下伊利沙伯二世，其儲君及繼任人，
並願遵守香港法律，維護法綱，執行法紀，勵
行職守，秉公行事，不枉不徇，並絕對服從上
級一切合法命令。』

(J.A. Finch)
Commandant,
Police Training School
警察訓練學校
校長

11th October 1976

Recruits swore their allegiance to Her Majesty the Queen on their
very first day in the Training School in the days of the Colony.

Every room of police building in the Colony was furnished with a
royal portrait inside.

Village gentry Chan Yiu-tsai, in traditional Chinese dress,
accompanied Governor Alexander Grantham in his Tai O visit during
the 1960s.

Members of the Rural Affairs Committee visited Tai O with
Governor and Madam Grantham in the sixties.

Anne, Princess Royal visited Tai O in 1971.

In 1985, U.S. President George H. W. Bush (L) visited the
British naval dock of Fenwick Pier, accompanied by Governor
Edward Youde (M) and Aide-de-camp Paul Collier (R).

Governor Christopher Patten and wife Lavender Thornton, 30
June 1997. Aide-de-camp Superintendent Lance Brown, back,
returned to the United Kingdom with Patten's departure.

Prince Charles with the Royal Escort Group during his visit to
Hong Kong in 1979.

(T) Autograph of Governor Patten with the Force Escort Group, 1997.

(B) The Force Escort Group, Tsing Ma Bridge, 1996.

Lady Ogilvy visiting the Police Driving School in 1986. Escort
missions used to be conducted by Traffic Division of the Hong
Kong Island District and members of the Police Driving School
before the Force Escort Group was established.

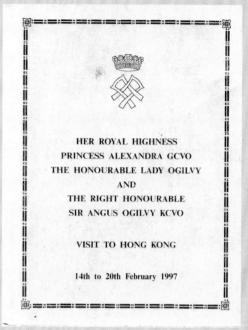

HER ROYAL HIGHNESS
PRINCESS ALEXANDRA GCVO
THE HONOURABLE LADY OGILVY
AND
THE RIGHT HONOURABLE
SIR ANGUS OGILVY KCVO

VISIT TO HONG KONG

14th to 20th February 1997

(Top left) Portrait of Lady Ogilvy, honorary Commandant of the RHKP, at the Gazetted Officer's Mess, Caine House, RHKP Headquarters.

(Top right, bottom) Itinerary of Lady Ogilvy's visit, February, 1997.

Police Award Ceremony, 1934.

HM Queen Elizabeth II, born on 21 April, observes an Official Birthday[22] that is marked by major celebrations, including the traditional Trooping the Colour (in which the sovereign takes the salute herself in a mounted inspection) and her bestowal of the Birthday Honours. In the early days, the colonial administration organized the annual celebrations at Government Stadium for both the Trooping and the Honours. Major roads nearby were closed on the day of the ceremonies so that larger armoured vehicles from the BFO could traverse the grounds easily. Districts and departments – Anti-riot, Women Officers, RPCs, Police Dog Unit, and so on – all sent representatives. The Governor himself donned official dress, ostrich plumes and all, in representation of his fellow colonial administrators as he awarded honours to outstanding members in the disciplinary forces as well as citizens who have contributed to the community.

When a RHKP officer's tenure reaches 18 years with good conduct, a Long Service Medal, or Oldie's Badge in Cantonese parlance, would usually be awarded. Above 24 years, a clasp or pip[23] was added to the ribbon (First Award). 30 years called for a Second clasp, and at 33 years of tenure a maximum of three stars were awarded. A few officers with two decades or more of outstanding service, usually at Superintendent rank or above, were awarded with the Colonial Police Medal for Meritorious Service (post-nominal CPM). Generally speaking, the Queen's Police Medal (QPM) was only awarded to Chief Superintendents or their superiors. While these medals were worth much in and of themselves, they conferred honour and recognition to the recipient officer.

The Annual Review and Honours ceremony were eventually moved from Government Stadium to other locations such as Central Police Station and Government House, with the Governor personally awarding and decorating citizens and public servants.

Long Service Medal Presentation, HKPF (L) and RHKP (R).

Police Review in Victoria City (Now Central and Western
District, and Wanchai District) during the 1920s. The fire brigade
was part of the Constabulary back then. The fire engine at the left
was transferred from the HKI Police Officers' Mess to the Police
Museum in 2004, when the Grand Station finally ceased service.

Chinese Inspector Chan Fook-cheung awarded by Governor Robert
Brown Black during the Annual Review at Government Stadium.
Standing behind the Governor was his aide-de-camp.

(T) Governor Geoffrey Northcote awarding honours at Central
Police Station, 11 April, 1939.

(B) Commissioner of Police Raymond Anning and Commandant of
Hong Kong Auxiliary Police Force (HKAPF) Chau Jiam-chiu
in an inspection with Governor Youde during the HKAPF's
1988 Annual Review.

Hong Kong Auxiliary Police Band.

55th Anniversary of the Hong Kong Police Band.

Inspections at Central Station at the dawn of the 19th century, in white formal dress.

21   Passing Out Parades and Guard of Honour

The final task for Probationary Inspectors (PI) and RPCs at Wong Chuk Hang Police Training School was the graduation drill known as the Passing Out Parade. Probationary Inspectors would lead squads of RPCs to the drill square, all to training officers' loud dictums and rowdy cheers from family and friends. At the Parade, the best performer in the RPC examinations was awarded the Silver Whistle[24], whereas the overall valedictorian received the Sutcliffe Cup. At the PI Course Inspectorate classes, the Brian Slevin Trophy went to the top student of the intake, and Batons of Honour were awarded to the best performers of each class.

As for incumbent officers at the PTU headquarters, a graduation ceremony was organized upon their completion of training. It differed from the Passing Out Parade at Wong Chuk Hang in the drill square: blue berets appeared in anti-riot formation, with their squad commanders standing on anti-riot armoured carrier vehicles for inspection by superior officers.

Every year the Force organized a Police Night/Guard of Honour, a tradition hailing from 16th century British castles where each garrisoned force played a bugle call[25] to summon the troops for the night before the gates were shut and the drawbridge went up. The custom evolved into a variety show of sorts in Hong Kong: at each Commissioner's retirement, war memorial, the start of the legal year (then Michaelmas term), a new Chief Justice arriving or assuming office, police anniversaries or any notable occasions, officers from different districts and units convened and marched to the accompanying tune of the Police Band.

When the Grand Station that was Central Police Station was about to be de-commissioned in 2004, a Guard of Honour was held at its compound to bid farewell to the historic complex. At the sesquicentennial anniversary of the RHKP in 1994, another one was held at Tamar. While the Police Night/Guard of Honour tradition thrives to this day, it is no longer an internal affairs, and ticket-holding citizens are now free to visit with all proceeds going to charity.

Police Night on the eve of de-commissioning of Central Police Station.

Passing Out Parade of graduate Marine Police officers at the
Wong Chuk Hang Police Training School, 1963.

Rifle drill for PIs and RPCs during a Passing Out Parade in the early eighties. PIs commanded at the front and RPCs followed.

Guard of Honour for the de-commissioning of Central Police
Station.

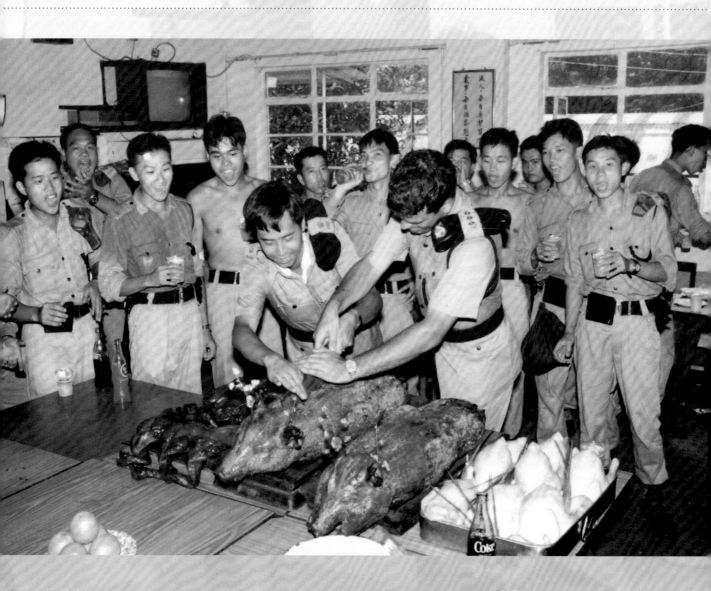

PTU Guanyu worship rituals, 1984.

22   Pai Kwan Tei (Worshipping the Military God)

Various police units in Hong Kong worshipped Guan Yu[26] as a matter of custom, with his likeness usually housed in the relatively spacious and frequented mess. 'Common rooms', where CID officers worked on their cases, also saw the Emperor's statue. The ones worshipped by the police[27] were usually standing upright holding the crescent poleblade that now bears his name, but seldom seen studying his military tomes. The shrine itself was placed with utmost care, never facing east, because that was precisely how he met his end with the ambush and decapitation by Ma Zhong, as Guan retreated westward to the city of Maicheng. Guan's blade must also never point at anyone who's 'one of us'.

While the custom might have existed before the war, it didn't really catch on until the fifties. Every now and then the units would perform the ritual, perhaps when a superior officer was leaving or a new one incoming, or colleagues' promotion, or difficulties at work, or after cracking a big case - all this and more. Colleagues would order a roasted pig, chicken, goose, and incense trinkets from the Cantonese barbecue restaurant with money in the kitty, and the restaurant would send skillful worker to take care of the rest at the station. The offerings depended on the status or severity of the event, with a minimum of one mid-sized pig, three chickens and three roast geese.

The commanding officer first lit three large joss sticks and burnt a paper offering of regal outfits to the Emperor on behalf of his colleagues, and then each would offer his own joss sticks. The commander and VIPs/promotees then carved the pig with a single cut from head to tail, and then the master barbecuer from the shop hacked up the rest. While some of the commanding officers were British, and other colleagues tended to be of various faiths, most of the time they joined in with the ceremony for the Emperor's sake. What began as a folk religion in China became a coalescing force amongst colleagues in each police unit.

While the Force still practises the custom from time to time, policing cultures have evolved and the ceremony now pales in contrast to the pomp and circumstance in the sixties and seventies. At Wong Tai Sin Police Station, both Guan Yu and the eponymous neighbourhood deity, Wong Tai-sin himself, are worshipped, albeit at different spots.

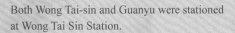
Both Wong Tai-sin and Guanyu were stationed at Wong Tai Sin Station.

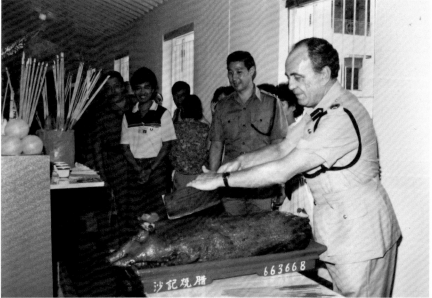

(T) Guanyu worship at the Police Driving School, 1970s.

(B) Marine CID in 1980s, with carver Marine District Commander J. P. Clark.

Guanyu ceremonies usually call for a minimum of one mid-sized
pig, three chickens and three roast geese.

Female inspectors in regal dress for Mess Night during the seventies.

23   Mess Night

The tradition of Mess Night was a formal affair in the British military, with requisite mess dress for its officers and strict rules and procedures throughout the banquet. The regimental dinner was picked up by their police compatriots and renamed Police Officers Mess Night. As a British-built and led institution, the RHKP also organized various regular and occasional Mess Nights during the colonial period as a matter of fraternity. With a western menu on offer, the dining-in had a good selection of wines throughout the courses. Police Training School (now Police College) hosted a Night for each PI intake and graduation at its own mess.

With the exception of specially invited guests, all attendees were officers who wore mess kits with miniaturized rank badges and medals. Civilian evening dress was only worn with special dispensation. Women police officers started out without a uniform mess kit and attended with their personal outfits, but now sport a top similar to those of their male colleagues alongside trousers or dress, a la Regina Ip when she became Commissioner of Immigration Department.

Mess Nights were known for the speeches by the celebrant and guests, who spoke not behind podiums or on stages but soaring on the dinner tables. Health and safety meant that chairs have become an acceptable alternative now. Around the end of the sixties, Police Training School added a curious segment to the rundown, with the shortest PI recruit, physically speaking, carrying a duck around in uniform and badge. Duck Major, as the (very much alive) bird was officially ranked, was taken around every table where it would receive a kiss from all female attendees.

Legend has it that a few PIs were having an evaluation session at Mong Kok Police Station in November of 1969, when Assistant Commissioner Russell White's pet duck darted out of the washroom that was its temporary quarters. Realizing that it was no foresighted strategy to keep ducks in loos, Assistant Commissioner White sent it to Director of Police Training School David Lloyd, ostensibly for some much-needed training because Lloyd boasted that his school could get ducks in a row. The custom premiered in January of the following year for some reasons and persevered to this day. With avian flu pandemics after the handover, mess nights now resort to wooden ducks.

The curious Duck Major of Mess Night.

(T) All attendees apart from specially invited guests were required to wear mess kits.

(B) Officers' and Working Partners' Luncheon at Officers' Mess, Tseung Kwan O Station, East Kowloon Regional Headquarters.

Then Chief Executive Donald Tsang as celebrant on Mess Night 2012, making his address on a table per longstanding custom.

Coppers' curries.

24   Curry Culture

The dish of spice and sauce, of meats and rice, of all South Asia: curry finds its home in Bangladesh, Nepal, Sri Lanka, India and Pakistan. Indian and later on Pakistani officers have served in the force since its inception in 1844, and they brought their culinary traditions along the way. How curry became a staple of police mess culture itself was a subtler affair.

As a disciplinary force with clear ranks and disparate benefits, the RHKP drew its boundaries down to the mess. Rank-and-file weren't allowed into officers' mess, and in the early days even had separate washrooms. The multi-ethnic force still segregated itself with white officers at the top and non-whites below, and the problem of race and rank impressed itself within the walls of each district and station.

What began as cuisine for a minority of Indian and Pakistani constables in the Force turned out to be palatable to every colour and creed, and some units started internal curry gatherings which drew colleagues of all backgrounds into a melting pot. With growing popularity, the occasional curry days became fixed, spreading from land forces to the marine police and even to other disciplinary forces such as the correctional services. Some district or station commanders went further than these regular meetings by introducing guests and friends to the dinners, making them more neighbourly than collegial.

The post of Police Cook, held by commissioned constables, was responsible for feeding the Force in the early days. They were instructed in various preparations of curry at the force Catering School. The PTU headquarters in Fanling had an enormous kitchen staffed by experienced Police Cooks whose premium curry dishes were renowned in the force. As these specialized posts dwindled in number, mess meals were gradually taken over by outside contractors, and what was once the curry custom in the Force now became the curry culture of Hong Kong.

Pakistani officers and their families in police quarters, 1960s. Curries were an integral part of their culinary tradition. (Courtesy of Information Services Department, HKSAR.)

Families Day, Wong Chuk Hang Police Training School, 1970s. (Courtesy of Information Services Department, HKSAR.)

25   Fraternity (Police Welfare Activities)

As the largest law enforcement agency in Hong Kong, the RHKP established a variety of institutions and social networking channels, within and without, over the years. As with the Bisley Shooting Contest in the county of Surrey, where military and civilian police officers competed in shooting ranges, Hong Kong ran its own annual Uniformed Police Shooting Contest with the Commissioner and officers in attendance.

The Force also offered various recreational and social facilities internally, running healthy activities for officers and their family members so that they would stick to the straight and narrow alongside their colleagues. One of these widely known events was the annual Dowman Road Race, a cross-country run held in February at Pak Tam Chung, Sai Kung, in commemoration of the running enthusiast Chief Inspector Christopher "Danny" Dowman. Participants had to complete some six to twelve kilometres, and everyone who made it to the finish line received a certificate as encouragement. More than 2,000 members of the Force joined the internal Race every year. Families Days were also held on a regular basis, with colleagues and family members making much mirth together.

Families Day, Police Training School, 1970s. (Courtesy of Information Services Department, HKSAR.)

Christmas Gala at Marine Police Headquarters, with (then child) actress Petrina Fung Bo-bo in tow.

Senior police officers and contestants of the British Army and Hong Kong Police Annual Shooting Contest outside Police Headquarters in 1957, in a tradition hailing from Bisley contests in the army. Then Commissioner of Police Arthur Maxwell, and Henry Heath, who would succeed him in two years' time, were both present. Pakistani officers stationed in New Territories wore a somewhat different uniform from the rest of the Force.

The Army and the Force at the San Po Kong military range in the 1957 annual contest. Police officers in New Territories uniform carried Lee Enfield .303 rifles. The winning team was awarded a prize by the Governor himself.

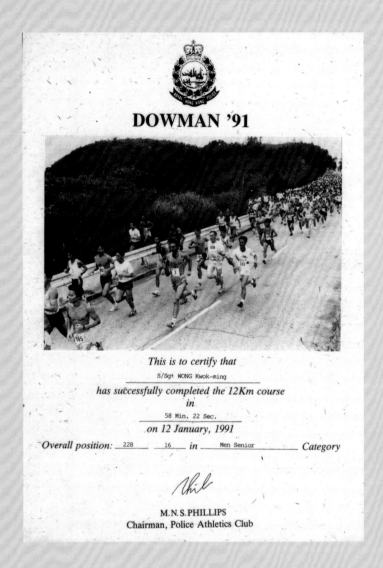

A 1991 Dowman Road Race certificate marking the completion
of the long-distance race.

Detail of the finishing line shot, 1991.

EUROPEAN INSPECTOR
SUMMER CEREMONIAL DRESS
HONG KONG POLICE
CIRCA 1915

CHINESE CONSTABLE
WINTER WORKING DRESS
HONG KONG POLICE
CIRCA 1930

GAZETTED OFFICER
WINTER CEREMONIAL DRESS
HONG KONG POLICE
CIRCA 1930

EUROPEAN SERGEANT
SUMMER WORKING DRESS
HONG KONG POLICE
CIRCA 1930

CHINESE SUB-INSPECTOR
SUMMER SERVICE DRESS
HONG KONG POLICE
CIRCA 1941

CHINESE CONSTABLE
HONG KONG POLICE
CIRCA 1858

SIKH CONSTABLE
WINTER WORKING DRESS
HONG KONG POLICE
CIRCA 1860

CHINESE CONSTABLE
WINTER WORKING DRESS
HONG KONG POLICE
CIRCA 1900

CHINESE CONSTABLE
SUMMER WORKING DRESS
HONG KONG POLICE
CIRCA 1900

INDIAN CONSTABLE
WINTER WORKING DRESS
HONG KONG POLICE
CIRCA 1900

INDIAN CONSTABLE
SUMMER WORKING DRESS
HONG KONG POLICE
CIRCA 1913

Figurines of early colonial police uniforms.

26   Uniforms

The uniformed police officers we see on patrol these days wear a light shade of blue, but in the 19th century they came in rifle green, and so officers came to be called greenclothes in Cantonese. With many Sikhs coming from India to join the service, wearing a dastar the size of a rice pot along with their uniforms, the somewhat jocular term of 'big-headed greenclothes'[28] became commonplace. Chinese officers were also called that, thanks to the pointed bamboo hats and police whistles they took on patrol. So ran a Cantonese nursery rhyme,

Big head'd greenclothes,
Division A, B, C, D goes.
Give him the slip
and his whistle blows.[29]

Hong Kongers who grew up in the sixties and seventies tend to remember those summer uniforms of green shorts and tube socks, not to mention the black baton and black leather boots. Only in 1977 did the Force phase out the short trousers in favour of long ones. Modern police officers are civilians and not soldiers, and the blue uniform is known throughout the western world; in using rifle green in its uniform, the Force signified paramilitary intent during the colonial period. A pale-blue all-weather uniform was rolled out in 2004, and the rifle green has now become a rare sight on the streets of Hong Kong, confined to Rural Patrol Units and Anti-Riot Units.

In some official occasions officers wear a whistle lanyard[30]. Back then the silver whistle came in handy when you needed to direct traffic or summon help, and it was kept in the chest pocket, often with the cord or lanyard. With improved communication devices, the cord fell out of use and sometimes became a hassle in emergency situations. It was finally abandoned in a Force Uniform and Accoutrements review in the nineties and became a purely ornamental award, as formally recognized by the Force or the government for outstanding service. The lanyard came in three varieties: the basic black, the tricolour (force colour) personally awarded by the Commissioner from 1993, and the red which was the highest ranked lanyard for the cream of the crop. Once bestowed by the Governor himself before the handover, it is now presented by the Chief Executive of the Hong Kong SAR.

Black, force colour, and red lanyards.

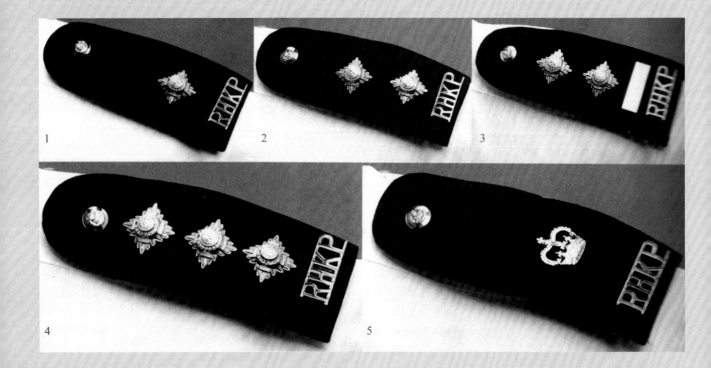

Pre-handover shoulder insignia / rank badge,
Royal Hong Kong Police.

1. Probationary Inspector

2. Inspector

3. Senior Inspector

4. Chief Inspector

5. Superintendent

6. Senior Superintendent

7. Chief Superintendent

8. Assistant Commissioner

9. Senior Assistant Commissioner

10. Deputy Commissioner

11. Commissioner

Summer working dress for Constables at the turn of the sixties, with impressive short trousers and tube socks. Officers wore yellow socks and were popularly known as yellowfin seabreams (*wong geuk laap*, lit. yellow legged breams). Rank and file officers wore black ones, hence black feet (*haak geuk*).

The shorts were laid to rest in 1977, but the black cane remained a potent symbol amongst police instructors and Chief Superintendent ranks or above. The Saxon, an armoured personnel carrier, was commissioned in a 1990s ceremony at Kai Tak Police Driving School, with School Director Stenton (with the sole silver staff) alongside British Army representatives.

Marine police uniform from various eras and posts. From left: 1990s uniform (identical to land police), craft unit uniform, winter and summer uniform from 1940s to 1970s, craft unit uniform. 1980s and 1960s launch duty uniform are at the far right and second right respectively.

Pale blue all-weather tops were instituted in 2004 for Sergeant
ranks. Station Sergeants or above wore white.

CID officers in the sixties.

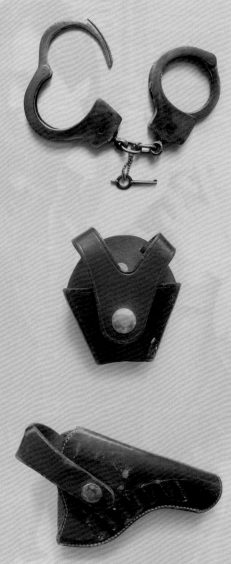

Plainclothes' own equipment in 1969: handcuffs, handcuff holders, and holster with clip.

27   Plainclothes Equipment

The Criminal Investigation Division is now popularly known as the CID or 'plainclothes'[31] rather than earlier Cantonese nicknames ranging from 'civvie-wear' to 'errand dispatches'[32]. CIDs today may find it hard to imagine a time back in the eighties when they had to buy and bring their own equipment to work for everything except the service revolver.

There were usually two kinds of handcuffs back in the day. The ones made with lightweight aircraft-grade antimony were imported and stamped with serial numbers for easy follow up in case of loss. These were sold at the Hong Kong Gun Shop on Pottinger Street, a bit expensive at a hundred dollars or so per pair. The other type was heavier and made of stainless steel and were sold for around forty dollars. Unbranded as they were, general nicknamed 'Sunshine Brand[33]'. It turns out that these were made by one Sunshine Hardware, a store on Circular Pathway near Ladder Street in Sheung Wan.

CIDs, old hands or otherwise, liked to get their holsters, handcuff holders, and clips at the 'Shanghai Bloke' on Jaffe Road. Both uniformed officers and CIDs carried the Colt Police .38e revolver with an extra-long barrel, which necessitated a holster with an open muzzle end. When a shorter-barreled pistol was issued to CIDs, the closed muzzle holster became the norm. Holsters could be tooled and carved to the officer's heart's content in those days for no more than a hundred dollars at the leather craftsmen in the basement of Wanchai's President Shopping Centre. Some CIDs had contacts with other shops and ordered custom holsters, cuff holders and clips, and few of them had identical equipment until the seventies.

The plainclothes policy was designed to ease investigation work, and detectives took a liking to short-sleeved Hawaiian shirts which were never tucked in – to better conceal their firearms and clips. The seventies also witnessed the boom of the safari-style, and as CIDs scrambled for tailors, the khaki bush jacket became an unofficial uniform for plainclothes.

Webley .38 Revolver.

1970s safari fashion amongst plainclothes officers.

CIDs in Hawaiian shirts transporting suspects in the seventies.

Triumph motorcycle combination with passenger rig (sidecar).

Rigs[34] have nothing to do with sailing. Properly known as motorcycle combinations or sidecars, the British postwar import was technically a motorcycle with a bucket seat attached to it.

These trikes were mainly used to take officers out on business rather than patrols. Senior Sergeants, the sixties/seventies equivalent of modern Station Sergeants, were quite powerful despite their middling official rank, and they were fond of these rides which inspired awe amongst the great unwashed.

It turns out that these rigs were not the easiest thing to drive, because the driver couldn't balance themselves with their left foot on the tarmac when braking, what with a seat in the way, and the whole rig would easily roll over on bumpy roads. While there was a horn to alert other drivers in an emergency, there were no police lights to catch others' attention. Still, rigs served in the Force until their gradual retirement in the seventies.

Jeeps, or lil' jeeps[35] as they were called in the service, were usually used for patrols or dispatches of anti-riot commanders. With four-wheel drive and plenty of horsepower, these police jeeps were well suited to hilly terrains and were widely deployed in remote districts. The one difficulty about driving a jeep was its stiff steering wheel, which took a lot of extra effort on the driver's part compared to other vehicles. Long retired by now, jeeps have been replaced by the Mitsubishi Pajero, with even more horsepower and easier handling.

For older Hong Kongers, the most striking scene was the use of 'pig lorries'[36] in arrests and subsequent transportation of unlicensed hawkers. The trailer was sealed in with chicken wire, and officers themselves were seated right in the middle or along the sides of the trailer, back to back or face to face. Sharp turns sometimes threw them right off their seats.

Triumph motorcycles, sometimes transliterated into Cantonese *caam fu pai*.

Hong Kong Traffic Police, 1925.

Female traffic officers riding scooters in 1960s. The vehicles were colloquially known as *min yeung tsai*, or lil' sheep.

(T) Police Jeep with silver paint in the fifties.

(B) Police Jeep for Communications and Logistics Units at the
     turn of the 1970s.

(T) Police Jeep on standby at Central Station in the eighties.

(B) Bomb disposal Unit Jeeps at the turn of the eighties.

(T) Austin patrol cars were used for traffic and anti-crime publicity in the early days.

(B) Earlier traffic patrol cars were painted in black and white, which earned them the nickname of panda cars.

(T) Patrol cars in current use.

(B) Electric vehicles used by the HKPF.

Alvis FV603 Saracen armoured personnel vehicles used by the
Force in the eighties.

(T) PTU Passing Out Parade in 1980s with Saracens on display.

(B) Armoured personnel vehicles modified from old lorries between the sixties and seventies, nicknamed *tou pau*, lit. native or earthen cannon.

(T) Large transport vehicles used by the police at the turn of the fifties.

(B) 'Pig lorries', or large transport vehicles (Heavy General Purpose) with chicken wire between the semi-trailer and the roof, used in the eighties and nineties.

The modern pig lorry, a Mercedes-Benz Vario Trooper nicknamed 'pork chop' or *chu pa*, as a homonym to Trooper.

A show of different types of police vehicles at Police Driving School at Shouson Hill.

Police launch in 1937.

29   Police Boats and Launches

When the Marine Police was established in 1842, the fleet comprised a few wooden sailboats, and some rowing was involved. The first batch of steamboat-sampans[37] were ordered in 1893 and marked the first steps to modernization. Most marine duties relied on them before WWII broke out, and subsequent orders proved even heavier and bulkier as each year passed. Steamboats were powered by a coal burning engine and firemen shoveled it into the burners constantly; they were employed as civilian technicians rather than police officers. These crafts were named 'Police No. 1', 'Police No. 2', and so on.

Petrol-powered crafts were commissioned from the fifties, and they were speedier and better equipped with custom marine designs: crafts intercepted smugglers while riverboats patrolled narrow, shallow waters. As the Marine Police grew into a modern unit of law enforcement, its Damen launches became integral to the fleet. They were hardy and durable as they brazed choppy seas at a top speed of 24 nmi/h (44km/h), and they were fuel efficient on slow patrols. Depending on the year they were laid down, Damens were divided into Mark I, II and III. The first two of these have since been phased out.

Each launch had its own ship identification number, but earlier ones had no Chinese names until the advent of Damen Mark II in the 1980s. At the invitation of the Marine Police, Prof. Chan Yiu-nam, then of the School of Chinese at the University of Hong Kong, named them after Confucian virtues. The seas of Hong Kong are now patrolled by the likes of *Police Benevolence*, *Police Justice*, *Police Propriety*, *Police Wisdom*, *Police Loyalty*, and *Police Piety*.

The present fleet has over 170 vessels on assorted duty, including marine patrol, border control, anti-smuggling interception, and search and rescue operations. Nowadays, the Hong Kong Marine Police is one of the biggest marine law enforcers in the world.

Police No. 26 sailing in winter of 1960 without so much as a windshield.

Police No. 1.

Police No. 30.

Mui Wo Station, 1970.

30   Police Posts and Quarters

Police posts

Since there is always a police station in the neighbourhood, urban dwellers seldom even catch sight of those little things. Police posts are far more familiar to residents in rural New Territories or the Outlying Islands. They are part and parcel of everyday life, and assistance from duty officers extends far beyond reporting crime. Back in the day, police posts along the border area also seconded as military outposts.

Such a post was erected in Pak Hok Chau between 1950 and 1951, a sturdy piece of rebar concrete with seven Constables and a Sergeant who went on duty for seven days straight before taking three off. Its proximity to the border required a defensive position with gun slits (embrasures) for armed constables. Searchlights installed atop the police post shone along the barbed-wire border fence.

As Hong Kong urbanized along with a maturing police force, much of the earlier facilities in Pak Hok Chau have been decommissioned. Other posts with ageing equipment or anachronistic locations were rebuilt or relocated. Lamma's post used to watch over the cliffs of Hung Shing Yeh beach, was relocated to newly reclaimed land at Yung Shue Wan with modern and environmentally friendly facilities. The HKPF still establishes new police posts when the need arises. Penny's Bay in northeast Lantau has been developed into a Disneyland resort, and Lantau division matched it with a themed police post that sat well with the rest of the architecture. Kai Tak Cruise Terminal also premiered a Police Post in 2013, and far from fading away into history, they continue to stand tall at Hong Kongers' service with an occasional fresh lick of paint.

Lee Chi Keung, stationing at Pak Hok Chau Police Post in 1965.

Former Chai Wan Police Post, now Tai Tam Scout Centre.

(T) Former Causeway Bay Police Station.

(B) Former Shau Kei Wan Police Station, now Traffic Accident Investigation Division, Hong Kong Island and Shau Kei Wan Police Reporting Centre.

Outside Hollywood Road Police Married Quarters in the sixties.

Quarters

Only European and British officers were housed in single or married quartered before WWII. Chinese rank-and-file bachelors lodged in station barracks, whereas their married colleagues resorted to private rentals with a monthly stipend of seven dollars. The Force decided to build police quarters after the war, and the first residences for married rank-and-file personnel in all Asia, Hollywood Road Police Married Quarters, were completed in 1951. More followed all over Hong Kong Island and Kowloon.

The early PMQs were managed with the strictness of barracks by a full-time Barracks Sergeant, and family members were subjected to some form of supervision as well. Stations from each police district sent constables to station at the quarters, with occasional inspections by officers. Any violations were dealt with as a disciplinary matter and could result in the relinquishment of the flat. Scores were kept for each application, depending on rank, years of service, number of family members and other compassionate grounds.

Inside Hollywood Road Quarters in 1974.

Residents were not allowed to keep pets – not even a bird or a goldfish. Only immediate family members could move in.

The earlier quarters had long wide corridors on each floor, with kitchen facilities along the way opposite the front door of the flats, and common washrooms and baths at each end of the corridor. Since all the residents were police families and everybody spent a lot of time in these communal spaces, neighbourly relations were warm and ever helpful. Quarters built after the eighties were designed with an emphasis on privacy, with each flat housing its facilities behind its own doors and minus the barracks-style management. These were virtually identical to any private apartment blocks, and the next door neighbour became less friendly.

Pre-rehabilitation, Hollywood Road PMQ.
(Courtesy of Albert Poon.)

Notes

Chapter One. The Force

1   A Multi-ethnic Force

    1   "An Ordinance for the preservation of good order and cleanliness within the Colony of Hong Kong". 20 March, 1844.

2   Aboard the Sampan

    2   Gendarmeries generally refer to military forces charged with police duties amongst civilian populations, during peacetime or otherwise. For details on the Japanese context in WWII, see Chapter Three.

3   Japanese Occupation

    3   Of the Imperial Japanese Army. Its naval counterpart, the *Tokkeitai*, operated in the South Pacific theatre.

    4   Chinese subordinates were called *hin cha*, Cantonese, lit. *kempei* (gendarmes) *junsa. Junsa*, Japanese for patrolman.

    5   *Otsukaresama deshita*, roughly translated as 'thank you for your hard work' with honorifics.

Chapter Two. The Training

6   Recruits

    6   Nicknamed *si ye*, or grandmaster, from Classical Chinese for mandarins' advisors.

9   Police Dog

    7   *Yu huen si.*

Chapter Three. Duty and Mission

10   Charge Room: Police Stations

    8   *"Saang bat yap gwoon moon, sei bat yap dei yuk."* Cantonese adage.

11   Warrants

    9   *Sau cha ling*, lit. search warrants, later shortened to *sau ling* and colloquially written in homophones, lit. hand warrants.

    10   Cap 232, Laws of Hong Kong, now consolidated in Cap 238 and 295.

    11   Cap 213, ibid.

    12   Cap 132, now Public Health and Municipal Services Ordinance.

    13   *hang wai bo*, lit. behaviour booklet, government jargon for divisional report file or DRF.

    14   Until 1949, with the introduction of the status Citizen of the United Kingdom and Colonies (which was in turn abolished in 1982). UK immigration control of CUKCs began in 1962.

12   Street Beat Patrols

    15   *Siu Lo Bo*, from the eponymous Japanese live-action drama series about a family robot, *Ganbare!! Robokon*, broadcast in Hong Kong in the seventies.

16   "Boat People": Vietnamese Refugees

    16   The term "Vietnamese boat people" is a widely used catchall for all refugees who fled the Vietnam War by sea.

17   Cross-border Crime

    17   *Daai huen jai*, lit. big loop kid. Organized criminal group. Etymology uncertain, ranging from tyre/buoys used by immigrants, the 'circle' of Canton conurbations on atlases, to esoteric triad oaths.

    18   *Saang gong kei bing*, lit. Banner Army of the (Guangdong/Canton) Province and the (Hong Kong) Harbour. The Banner Army was a reference to militarism by Manchu rulers over majority Han Chinese during the Qing dynasty.

Epilogue

As the Hong Kong Police Force steps into its 171st year of existence, in a digital era more sensitive to visuals and images than to words – a world which maintains that "seeing is believing" – we opted for the pictorial instead of the textual. With retired police officers loaning us their precious private collections, we aim to guide our readers on a journey of police development in Hong Kong, pointing out the little things in training, service, buildings, and protocol along the way which gradually add up over the century to make the Force what it is today.

The assistance and support from two retired police officers' associations were instrumental to our trawl for information over the last few years: we eventually collected hundreds of photographs and documents related to police work. The treasure trove of information came from all ranks, years, and posts, ranging from museum-worthy postcards and prim and proper group photos to some striking poses by officers in various settings; but the most exceptional of them all are those taken off-duty in collegial gatherings, never published until now. It is this panorama of work and life which truly informs us of the singular subculture in the largest government department through a vivid illustration of its major transformations. As we pored over the photographs and manuscript, it became apparent to us that the culture of the Force can be summed up in four words: discipline, obedience, cohesion, and fraternity. We hope our readers can piece together the sum of these parts in the photographs across the sections.

Of the three authors, two are involved in the academic discipline of police administration, whereas the third is a police history enthusiast who had himself served in the Force for some thirty years. We are of the conviction that the developmental history of the HKPF, as an integral component of the wider history of Hong Kong, will fall short of a full narrative if it is wholly penned by scholars without frontline policing experience, or alternatively handled by those assigned by the Force to the exclusion of others. We hope that this cooperation between officers and academics will build a fuller picture for those who are interested in the subject of police forces.

On a final note of thanks, we would like to express our gratitude for our very unassuming and bashful sources who joked that they were "utterly unimportant" offhand. This book was only made possible by your generous loan of materials, your long-suffering clarifications, and your enthusiastic referrals to other retired officers for interviews. Your tales may not have been the most arresting ones against the backdrop of turbulent times, but your testimony is without a doubt a treasure to serving officers and all of us who are keen to understand the past and present of the Hong Kong Police Force.

Acknowledgments (Names listed in no particular order)

A book such as this would not be possible without the advice, assistance and encouragement of many people. The writers would like to thank the following ladies/gentlemen and organizations for their support and contributions:

Retired Police Officers
Mr FUNG Siu-yuen Gordon
Mr KOO Si-hung Henrique
Mr CHAN Wai-ki
Mr David Hodson
Mr James ELMS
Mr Ian STENTON
Ms CHU Siu-hung
Mr YIP Pau-fuk, RIP
Mr NG Chuen-chung
Mr YAU Sui-hang

Hong Kong Police Old Comrades' Association
Mr CHAN Fook-cheung
Mr AU Ting
Mr MAK Kwai-shing Raymond
Mr TAM Kwong-choy
Mr WONG Kwok-ming
Mr YIP Mak
Ms KWOK Siu-fung
Mr WONG Chung-kei
Mr TANG Yau-shing
Mr LEE Chi-keung
Mr LEE Chiu-man
Mr LI Kam-wah
Ms LAM Oi-sze
Mr SIU Chun-ming
Mr LAI Kam-kwong, RIP
Mr KWOK Chi-keung Herold
Mrs FONG Yip Ching-sin
Mr YIP Wai

Hong Kong Marine Police Retirees' Association
Mr LAI Wun-wing
Mr LOK Tak-chi Henry
Mr CHEUNG Shek-hung
Mr WAN Sing-fai
Mr LO Ping-chuen
Mr TONG Sing-yiu
Mr LUI Ching
Ms HUNG Wai-lan
Mr WONG Shu-hoi

Research Assistants
Miss CHAN Oi-ting Yolanda
Mr CHENG Wing Wingo
Mr WONG Kin-fung

Student Assistants
Miss WONG Sze-ki Vikki
Mr YUNG Chun Kit
Miss WAN Lei-shan Sandy
Miss LO Wai-ying Cathine
Miss MAN Kwan-ki Pandus
Mr KO Cheuk-yi
Miss LEUNG Wai-yee Grace
Mr HUI Reckmorrow

Others
Ms CHAN Wai-fun
Mr HO Kwok-kwan Kenneth
Ms MO Suet-yee Sherry
Miss HO Hui-yee Pan
Mr YEUNG Ying-chuen
Ms KAM Lai-yue
Mr IP Lap-ngai
Mr YING Hung-lun
Mr SZE Chun-cheong
Mr SHAM Chong-mun
Mr CHENG Ping-wah, RIP

Organizations
Hong Kong Police Force
Hong Kong Police Force Museum
Hong Kong Police Force Library
Hong Kong Police Philatelic Club
Sing Tao News Corporation Limited
Public Records Office